THE LITTLE BOOK OF
HOPE

MIX
Paper | Supporting
responsible forestry
FSC® C020056
www.fsc.org

Parts of this book were first published in 2020 by Trigger,
an imprint of Shaw Callaghan Ltd.

This expanded edition published in 2023 by OH! an Imprint of
Welbeck Non-Fiction Limited, part of Welbeck Publishing Group.
Based in London and Sydney.
www.welbeckpublishing.com

Compilation text © Welbeck Non-Fiction Limited 2023
Design © Welbeck Non-Fiction Limited 2023

Disclaimer:

ISBN 978-1-80069-348-7

Original compilation: Trigger
Editorial: Victoria Denne
Design: Fusion Graphic Design Ltd
Project manager: Russell Porter
Production: Jess Brisley

A CIP catalogue record for this book is available from the British Library

Printed in China

10 9 8 7 6 5 4 3 2 1

THE LITTLE BOOK OF

HOPE

FOR WHEN LIFE
GETS A LITTLE TOUGH

CONTENTS

INTRODUCTION

Modern life can be filled with so much: from the daily commute, a hectic schedule, cooking an evening meal, to those crucial turning points: quitting your job, moving house, finding love. Between the noise, it can be easy to lose hope, even when on the surface, things are going well.

The Little Book of Hope offers a little guidance for when the scales of life are tipped, times become turbulent and hope is in short supply. From the minds of some of the world's most well-known figures, learn to find your footing, take a breath and look to the future more positively.

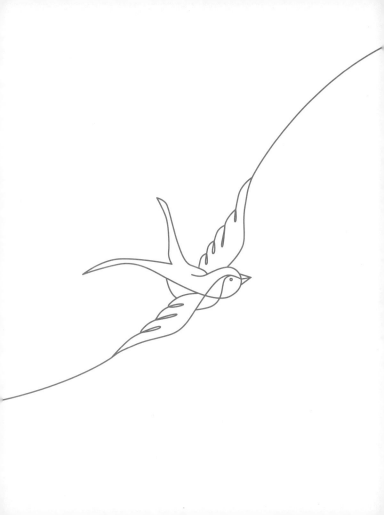

CHAPTER

1

WHEN YOU NEED A PUSH

Sometimes we just need a
little extra oomph to get us over
the finish line, or even to make it
to the end of the day.

The best way to not feel hopeless is to get up and do something. Don't wait for good things to happen to you. If you go out and make some good things happen ...

... you will fill the world with hope, you will fill yourself with hope.

Barack Obama

It's not the absence of fear, it's overcoming it. Sometimes you've got to blast through and have faith.

Emma Watson

Courage is not having the strength
to go on; it is going on when you
don't have the strength.

Theodore Roosevelt

Hope is that thing inside us that insists, despite all the evidence to the contrary, that something better awaits us if we have the courage to reach for it ...

... and to work for it and to fight for it.

Barack Obama

It is difficult to say what is impossible, for the dream of yesterday is the hope of today and the reality of tomorrow.

Robert H. Goddard

When life gets you down do you
wanna know what you've gotta do?
Just keep swimming.

Dory, *Finding Nemo* (2003)

Oft hope is born when all is forlorn.

J.R.R. Tolkien, *The Return of the King*

Perseverance is failing 19 times
and succeeding the 20th.

Julie Andrews

Through perseverance many people
win success out of what seemed
destined to be certain failure.

Benjamin Disraeli

Perseverance is more prevailing than violence; and many things which cannot be overcome when they are together, yield themselves up when taken little by little.

Plutarch

If you are going through hell, keep going.

Winston S. Churchill

Start by doing what's necessary;
then do what's possible; and suddenly
you're doing the impossible.

Francis of Assisi

Let me tell you the secret that
has led to my goal. My strength
lies solely in my tenacity.

Louis Pasteur

The man who moves a mountain begins
by carrying away small stones.

Confucius

What would happen if we were all brave enough to be a little bit more ambitious? I think the world would change.

Reese Witherspoon

I am a slow walker, but I never walk back.

Abraham Lincoln

He who believes is strong;
he who doubts is weak.
Strong convictions precede
great actions.

Louisa May Alcott

Knowing what must be done
does away with fear.

Rosa Parks

Never give out while there is hope;
but hope not beyond reason, for that
shows more desire than judgement.

William Penn

What would the hero of your life's movie
do right now? Do that.

Joe Rogan

It does not matter how slowly you go,
as long as you do not stop.

Confucius

I was taught the way of progress
is neither swift nor easy.

Marie Curie

It's perseverance that's the key.
It's persevering for long enough to
achieve your potential.

Lynn Davies

If you don't get out of the box you've been raised in, you won't understand how much bigger the world is.

Angelina Jolie

Hope is patience with the lamp lit.

Tertullian

Rivers know this: there is no hurry.
We shall get there some day.

A.A. Milne, *Winnie-the-Pooh*

There is nothing like a dream to
create the future.

Victor Hugo

A wise man will make more
opportunities than he finds.

Francis Bacon

CHAPTER
2

WHEN NOTHING'S GOING YOUR WAY

If you feel like life is stacked against you, don't despair: these words of wisdom will help you see things in a new light.

Keep the faith, don't lose
your perseverance and always
trust your gut extinct.

Paula Abdul

Our greatest glory is not in never falling,
but in rising every time we fall.

Confucius

When things go wrong,
don't go with them.

Elvis Presley

When you're at the end of your rope,
tie a knot and hold on.

Theodore Roosevelt

I gotta keep breathing.
Because tomorrow the sun
will rise. Who knows what
the tide could bring?

Chuck Noland, *Cast Away* (2000)

We must pass through the darkness,
to reach the light.

Albert Pike

You do not need to know precisely what is happening, or exactly where it is all going. What you need is to recognize the possibilities and challenges offered by the present moment, and to embrace them with courage, faith and hope.

Thomas Merton

The natural flights of the human mind
are not from pleasure to pleasure,
but from hope to hope.

Samuel Johnson

The past is a source of knowledge, and
the future is a source of hope. Love of the
past implies faith in the future.

Stephen Ambrose

You may encounter many defeats, but you must not be defeated. In fact, it may be necessary to encounter the defeats, so you can know who you are, what you can rise from, how you can still come out of it.

Maya Angelou

Every strike brings me closer
to the next home run.

Babe Ruth

Strange as it may seem, I still hope
for the best, even though the best,
like an interesting piece of mail, so
rarely arrives, and even when it does
it can be lost so easily.

Lemony Snicket, *The Beatrice Letters*

The most glorious moments in your
life are not the so-called days of
success, but rather those days when
out of dejection and despair ...

... you feel rise in you a challenge to life.

Gustave Flaubert

Many of life's failures are people
who did not realize how close they were
to success when they gave up.

Thomas Edison

All things are difficult before they are easy.

Thomas Fuller

Hope itself is like a star – not to be seen in the sunshine of prosperity, and only to be discovered in the night of adversity.

Charles Spurgeon

Failure is a great teacher and,
if you are open to it, every mistake
has a lesson to offer.

Oprah Winfrey

There should be no boundaries
to human endeavour. We are all
different. However bad life may
seem, there is always something
you can do, and succeed at.
While there's life, there is hope.

Stephen Hawking

To love means loving the unlovable.
To forgive means pardoning the
unpardonable. Faith means believing the
unbelievable. Hope means hoping when
everything seems hopeless.

G.K. Chesterton

Never lose hope. Storms make people stronger and never last forever.

Roy T. Bennett, *The Light in the Heart*

The greater the obstacle, the more
glory in overcoming it.

Molière

When you have lost hope, you have lost everything. And when you think all is lost, when all is dire and bleak, there is always hope.

Pittacus Lore, *I Am Number Four*

Sometimes even to live
is an act of courage.

Seneca

The road that is built in hope is more pleasant to the traveller than the road built in despair, even though they both lead to the same destination.

Marion Zimmer Bradley, *The Fall of Atlantis*

The future rewards those who press on. I don't have time to feel sorry for myself. I don't have time to complain. I'm going to press on.

Barack Obama

Out of difficulties grow miracles.

Jean De La Bruyère

Hope is like the sun, which,
as we journey toward it, casts the
shadow of our burden behind us.

Samuel Smiles

We are stronger in the places
we have been broken.

Ernest Hemingway

It's important for you to understand
that your experience facing and
overcoming adversity is actually one
of your biggest advantages.

Michelle Obama

There is no better than adversity.
Every defeat, every heartbreak,
every loss, contains its own seed,
its own lesson on how to improve
your performance the next time.

Malcolm X

My attitude is that if you push me
towards something that you think is
a weakness, then I will turn that
perceived weakness into a strength.

Michael Jordan

I learned compassion from being discriminated against. Everything bad that's ever happened to me has taught me compassion.

Ellen DeGeneres

He who has health, has hope;
and he who has hope, has everything.

Thomas Carlyle

CHAPTER

3

WHEN LOVE GETS YOU DOWN

Whether you've loved and lost
or are still waiting for the
right one to arrive, soothe your
heartache with these sage
words of advice.

Forgiveness provides hope, joy, and a
bright future that nothing else can.

Paul J. Meyer

It's a good place when all you have
is hope and not expectations.

Danny Boyle

Let your hook be always cast. In the pool where you least expect it, will be fish.

Ovid

Rules for happiness: something to do,
someone to love, something to hope for.

Immanuel Kant

Patience is the art of hoping.

Luc De Clapiers

We live by admiration, hope and love.

William Wordsworth

Love recognizes no barriers. It jumps hurdles, leaps fences, penetrates walls to arrive at its destination full of hope.

Maya Angelou

All human wisdom is summed up
in two words; wait and hope.

Alexandre Dumas

Life is meaningless only if we allow it to be. Each of us has the power to give life meaning, to make our time and our bodies and our words into instruments of love and hope.

Thomas Head Raddall

How far would you go to keep
the hope of love alive?

Nicholas Sparks

Hope is the dream of a waking man.

Aristotle

Hope guides me. It is what gets me through the day and especially the night. The hope that after you're gone from my sight it will not be the last time I look upon you.

A Knight's Tale (2001)

We need never be hopeless because we can never be irreperably broken.

John Green, *Looking for Alaska*

You can never leave footprints that last if you are always walking on tiptoes.

Leymah Gbowee

Faith has to do with things that
are not seen and hope with things
that are not at hand.

Thomas Aquinas

You don't lose hope, love.
If you lose hope,
you lose everything.

Mrs Potts, *Beauty and the Beast* (1991)

Mama always said life was like
a box of chocolates. You never
know what you're gonna get.

Forrest, *Forrest Gump* (1994)

To wish was to hope, and to
hope was to expect.

Jane Austen

We're all travelling through time together, every day of our lives. All we can do is do our best to relish this remarkable ride.

Tim, *About Time* (2013)

Beginnings are scary, endings are usually sad, but it is the middle that counts the most. You need to remember that when you find yourself at the beginning. Just give hope a chance to float up.

Birdee, *Hope Floats* (1998)

Just because you fail once doesn't mean you're gonna fail at everything.

Marilyn Monroe

The most common form of despair
is not being who you are.

Søren Kierkegaard

You call it hope – that fire of fire!
It is but agony of desire.

Edgar Allan Poe

If it were not for hopes,
the heart would break.

Thomas Fuller

The best way to predict the
future is to create it.

Abraham Lincoln

Whenever you are blue or lonely or stricken by some humiliating thing you did, the cure and the hope is in caring about other people.

Diane Sawyer

CHAPTER
4

WHEN YOU NEED A LIFT

Turn low moments into
high points with these inspiring
words of encouragement
and positivity.

This new day is too dear, with its
hopes and invitations, to waste a
moment on the yesterdays.

Ralph Waldo Emerson

Once you choose hope, anything's possible.

Christopher Reeve

Ever since happiness heard your
name, it has been running through
the streets trying to find you.

Hafiz of Persia

If winter comes, can spring be far behind?

Percy Bysshe Shelley

Do not spoil what you have by desiring what you have not; remember that what you now have was once among the things you only hoped for.

Epicurus

All our dreams can come true, if we
have the courage to pursue them.

Walt Disney

It's amazing how a little tomorrow can make up for a whole lot of yesterday.

John Guare, *Landscape of the Body*

Hope smiles from the threshold
of the year to come, whispering
'it will be happier'.

Alfred Tennyson

I finally started to let that go and
embrace my own type of beauty.
Everyone's bodies are different, and
we all have different shapes ...

... but it has nothing to do with
who you are.

Camila Mendes

This is where it all begins.
Everything starts here, today.

David Nicholls, *One Day*

He who plants a tree, plants a hope.

Lucy Larcom

Hope is the thing with feathers
That perches in the soul
And sings the tune without the words
And never stops at all.

Emily Dickinson

Everything that is done in this
world is done by hope.

Martin Luther

In the midst of winter, I find
within me the invisible summer.

Leo Tolstoy

The very things that hold you
down are going to lift you up.

Timothy Mouse, *Dumbo* **(1941)**

True hope is swift, and flies
with swallow's wings.

William Shakespeare

Hope is like the sun. If you only
believe it when you see it you'll never
make it through the night.

Princess Leia, *Star Wars: Episode VIII –
The Last Jedi* (2017)

Stop acting so small. You are
the universe in ecstatic motion.

Rumi

Dream as if you'll live forever,
live as if you'll die today.

James Dean

Hope in the face of difficulty.
Hope in the face of uncertainty.
The audacity of hope! In the
end, that is God's greatest gift to
us, the bedrock of this nation. A
belief in things not seen. A belief
that there are better days ahead.

Barack Obama

Every day is the opportunity
for a better tomorrow.

Nix, *Tomorrowland* (2015)

But if we hope for what we do not see, we wait with endurance.

Romans 8:25

Hope.

It's like a drop of honey, a field of tulips blooming in the springtime. It's a fresh rain, a whispered promise, a cloudless sky, the perfect punctuation mark at the end of a sentence. And it's the only thing in the world keeping me afloat.

Tahereh Mafi, *Unravel Me*

Hope is sweet-minded and sweet-eyed.
It draws pictures; it weaves fancies;
it fills the future with delight.

Henry Ward Beecher

Hope can be a powerful force. Maybe there's no actual magic in it, but when you know what you hope for most and hold it like a light within you, you can make things happen, almost like magic.

Laini Taylor, *Daughter of Smoke & Bone*

Where there's life, there's hope.

Theocritus

This new day is too dear,

with its hopes and invitations,

to waste a moment on the yesterdays.

Ralph Waldo Emerson, *Collected Poems and Translations*

CHAPTER
5

WHEN THE WORLD SEEMS BLEAK

If you find yourself
despairing of the world, remember:
the rainbow is there if you
look for it, you just have to see
past the rain.

The arc of the moral universe is long,
but it bends toward justice.

Martin Luther King Jr.

Yes, evil often seems to surpass good.
But then, in spite of us, and without
our permission, there comes at last an
end to the bitter frosts. One morning
the wind turns, and there is a thaw.
And so I must still have hope.

Vincent van Gogh

It is hope that gives life meaning.
And hope is based on the prospect of
being able one day to turn the actual
world into a possible one that looks better.

François Jacob

Hope is the only thing stronger than fear.

President Snow, *The Hunger Games* (2012)

You must not lose faith in humanity.
Humanity is an ocean; if a few drops of
the ocean are dirty ...

... the ocean does not become dirty.

Mahatma Gandhi

Children are the world's most valuable
resource and its best hope for the future.

John F. Kennedy

Bunty: Face the facts, ducks. The chances of us getting out of here are a million to one.
Ginger: Then there's still a chance.

Chicken Run (2000)

You can cut all the flowers but you
cannot keep spring from coming.

Pablo Neruda

There is a crack in everything.
That's how the light gets in.

Leonard Cohen, *Selected Poems, 1956-1968*

When the unthinkable happens,
the lighthouse is hope.

Christopher Reeve

Such is hope, heaven's own gift to
struggling mortals, pervading, like
some subtle essence from the skies,
all things both good and bad.

Charles Dickens

Hope is being able to see that there
is light despite all of the darkness.

Desmond Tutu

My hope still is to leave the world a bit better than when I got here.

Jim Henson

Without hope there's
no point to anything.

Marion, *Croupier*

Courage is like love; it must have
hope for nourishment.

Napoleon Bonaparte

I hope the fathers and mothers
of little girls will look at them
and say 'yes, women can'.

Dilma Rousseff

Hope allows us to push forward, even when the truth is distorted by the people in power. It allows us to stand up when they tell us to sit down, and to speak when they say be quiet.

Bryan Stevenson, *Just Mercy*

Even in the mud and scum of things,
something always, always sings.

Ralph Waldo Emerson

You can imprison a man, but not an idea.
You can exile a man, but not an idea.
You can kill a man, but not an idea.

Benazir Bhutto

Education is the passport to the
future, for tomorrow belongs to those
who prepare for it today.

Malcolm X

One child, one teacher, one book,
one pen can change the world.

Malala Yousafzai

Hope is like a road in the country; there was never a road, but when many people walk on it, the road comes into existence.

Lin Yutang

It's really a wonder that I haven't dropped all my ideals, because they seem so absurd and impossible to carry out. Yet I keep them, because in spite of everything, I still believe that people are really good at heart.

Anne Frank, *The Diary of a Young Girl*

Fairy tales do not tell children the dragons exist. Children already know that dragons exist. Fairy tales tell children the dragons can be killed.

G.K. Chesterton

He who has a why to live for can bear
almost any how.

Friedrich Nietzsche

So dry your tears. The storm has not yet
broken upon you with too much violence.
Your anchors are holding firm ...

... and they permit you both comfort in the present, and hope in the future.

Boethius

To plant a garden is to
believe in tomorrow.

Audrey Hepburn

But what we call our despair is often only
the painful eagerness of unfed hope.

George Eliot

CHAPTER

6

WHEN ALL ELSE FAILS

When there is nothing else,
remember:
there is always hope.

In all things, it is better to hope
than to despair.

Johann Wolfgang von Goethe

The miserable have no other
medicine, but only hope.

William Shakespeare

To live without hope is to cease to live.

Fyodor Dostoyevsky

May your choices reflect your
hopes, not your fears.

Nelson Mandela

Hope is passion for what is possible.

Søren Kierkegaard

A leader is a dealer in hope.

Napoleon Bonaparte

Make the most of moments that matter.

Kate Middleton, Duchess of Cambridge

I hope I can be as good of a father to my son as my dad was to me.

Calvin Johnson

Youth is easily deceived because
it is quick to hope.

Aristotle

The very least you can do in your life is figure out what you hope for. And the most you can do is live inside that hope. Not admire it from a distance but live right in it, under its roof.

Barbara Kingsolver, *Animal Dreams*

With high hope for the future, no prediction is ventured.

Abraham Lincoln

The great moral powers of the
soul are faith, hope, and love.

Ellen G. White

Don't judge each day by the harvest you
reap but by the seeds that you plant.

Robert Louis Stevenson

Hopeful, we are halfway to where we want
to go; hopeless, we are lost forever.

Lao Tzu

I like the immaterial world. I like to live among thoughts and images of the past and the possible, and even of the impossible, now and then.

Thomas Love Peacock

I thought that the light-house
looked lovely as hope, that star
on life's tremulous ocean.

Thomas Moore

Hope is nature's veil for
hiding truth's nakedness.

Alfred Nobel

Hope is the struggle of the soul,
breaking loose from what is perishable,
and attesting her eternity.

Herman Melville

The unknown future rolls toward us. I face it, for the first time, with a sense of hope. Because if a machine, a Terminator, can learn the value of human life, maybe we can too.

Sarah Connor, *Terminator 2: Judgment Day* (1991)

Hope is a good breakfast,
but it is a bad supper.

Francis Bacon

Fear can hold you prisoner.
Hope can set you free.

Red, *The Shawshank Redemption* (1994)

Sometimes I can only groan, and suffer, and pour out my despair at the piano.

Frédéric Chopin

Even if I knew that tomorrow
the world would go to pieces,
I would still plant my apple tree.

Martin Luther

Kirk: We got no ship, no crew, how're going to get out of this one?
Spock: We will find hope in the impossible.

Star Trek Beyond (2016)

Hope is a good thing, maybe the best of
things, and no good thing ever dies.

Andy, *The Shawshank Redemption* **(1994)**